AF589992

care
fully
ASHLI SOWELS-FIELDS, LPC
METICULOUS QUESTIONS
SUPPORTIVE AFFIRMATIONS
& MINDFUL PROMPTS
FOR YOUR GUIDED
SELF-CARE JOURNEY
SELF-CARE
DESIGNED
DELIBERATELY

For
Mrs. Lilly

Introduction

In order to "do self-care," you must know self... yourself. You must understand your needs, wants, values, beliefs, vulnerabilities, and how you manage the challenges that sometimes get in the way. There's only so much information you can get from Google and all the social media universities. The best source of information is **YOU**!

This journal was created to give you an opportunity to go deep within yourself, explore, discover, and come up with the best way to take care of you! You'll get a little help from me with questions, prompts, and supportive affirmations, but this is YOUR journey... YOUR design... YOUR version of self-care.

Remember, this is a personal and intimate journey. Give yourself time and space to sit with your discoveries.

Explore with compassion... discover with understanding... take a break... repeat!

The Layout

Throughout the journal, you will find meticulous questions, supportive affirmations, and mindful prompts to design your version of self-care.

Meticulous Questions

These pages will offer self-examining questions that will help you delve into yourself to learn and understand the best way for you to take care of you. There are two questions per page. The first question sets the mood, and the second...well, you'll see.

Supportive Affirmations

There are a total of 200 affirmations. There are 100 complete affirmations and 100 that are fill-in-the-blank style. Creating and maintaining your personal style of self-care is no easy feat. You may come across questions that you don't want to answer, that you can't easily answer, or that have multiple answers, and that's okay. I encourage you to use the affirmations when you need the support (whatever that looks like for you).

Mindful Prompts

Each journal prompt gives you the space to acknowledge ways in which you take care of yourself in real time. Sometimes we forget or dismiss our small wins; you should be able to acknowledge those things in real time, no matter how big or small.

______________________ CARE

"YOUR NAME"

When I open this journal, I will do so with compassion, grace, gratitude, love, understanding, and ______________ (what would you like to add?). I will release judgment, negative criticism, and ____________ (what would you like to add?). I will honor my commitment to myself. This one here is for me!

Allow the statements above to settle in and begin when you're ready. You can start on the first page, the last page, or anywhere in between. Do you!

Do you find it difficult
to take time for
yourself even when
you know you need it?

How do you convince yourself
that something/someone
is more important than you
and/or your well-being?

I DESERVE HONESTY FROM MYSELF.

I will not reduce myself to

____

How often do you
take time for yourself?

What does taking time
for yourself mean?

I WILL HEAL
WITHOUT
CONDITIONS.

I am
capable of

____

Do you push off your needs/wants until the end of your day only to have them unfulfilled because you've given your mental, physical, emotional, and spiritual energy to something/someone else?

What are those needs/wants?
How do you convince yourself that those needs/wants "can wait"?

I WILL
SATURATE
MYSELF
WITH
KINDNESS.

Today I will operate in

____

What tends to motivate your self-care?

Is it ever motivated by shame, fear, or guilt?
Is it proactive? Is it reactive?

I HAVE
THE ABILITY
TO ADJUST.

My voice is

Self-talk is what you say to yourself about yourself. Describe your self-talk.

Are there circumstances or situations where a change in self-talk would be beneficial? Describe the circumstance or situation and what your self-talk could sound like.

MY
FEELINGS
MATTER.

My efforts are

____

What's your perception of yourself?
Feel free to be as honest
and raw as you'd like.

Look at your response.
Is this your true perception of you?
Or is this the world's perception of you?
Or perhaps your parents, an ex, a child... ?

I AM
CAPABLE OF
SAYING NO
WITHOUT
GUILT.

I give myself permission to

____

Does your body ever tell you
you're doing too much or not enough?

When? Do you listen?
Do you ignore your body?
Why? Why not?

MY
EXPERIENCE
MATTERS.

I can respond to my emotions with

____

What are your daily basic needs?
(Ex: food, water, toilet)

Which of your needs gets regularly sacrificed?
What do they get sacrificed for?

I WILL MAKE SPACE FOR MYSELF IN ROOMS THAT WERE NOT ORIGINALLY CREATED FOR ME.

I can fill my mind with

____

Recall a time when you needed emotional support and your friend, partner, child, family member simultaneously needed emotional support from you. What did you do? How did you feel?

How do you verbalize your needs in your familial, platonic, romantic, and professional relationships?

I WILL
MAKE SPACE
FOR MY
THOUGHTS,
FEELINGS,
AND
EXPERIENCES.

Today
I will
choose

Recall a moment when you said "yes" but wanted to say "no."

Was that choice less about saying "yes" to the task and more about how you'd be perceived if you said "no"? Explain.

MY
SELF-
VALIDATION
IS ENOUGH.

I have the option to

____

Do you navigate or
push through challenging moments?
What does "navigating" look like for you?
What does "pushing through" look like?

What needs/wants are being sacrificed
when you "push through"?

I DON’T HAVE TO BE STRONG EVERY MOMENT OF EVERY DAY.

I will use this moment to focus my attention on

____

When things are going well in your life, are you fully present? Describe.

Do you often miss out on the fullness of some moments because you're "waiting for the other shoe to drop" (anticipating something going wrong or something bad happening)? Explain.
What would it be like to be more present?

IF I HAVE
MOMENTS
WHEN I DON'T
FEEL STRONG,
IT DOESN'T
HAVE TO MEAN
ANYTHING.
I CAN BE
PRESENT WITH
JUST THAT.

I am more than just

____

Does it sometimes seem like your thoughts are dragging you all over the place? Describe.

What might it look like or sound like if you were more aggressive and/or defiant toward some of those thoughts?

MY
EMOTIONS
ARE JUST
THAT...
MY
EMOTIONS.

I accept
that I

Recall a time when you had to update one of your devices because of a faulty system, an outdated system, or the system just needed to be upgraded with new features. Is your self-care system in need of an update? Explain.

How could you update your self-care system? Be as detailed as possible.

"NO"
IS ALWAYS
AN OPTION.

I can
take care
of myself
even
if/when

____

What parts of you get neglected?
Why? How?

What could happen if you gave those parts a little time and attention?

IT'S
OKAY
IF I TAKE
A BREAK.

I will
allow

What's your relationship with rest and recovery?

What's your relationship with rest and recovery particularly after challenging or adverse situations?

I CAN
USE THIS
MOMENT TO
CONSIDER
WHAT'S
BEST
FOR ME.

I will
not
allow

What's your relationship with control?

What could you do with the mental, physical, and/or emotional space that might appear if you relinquished control of at least some of those things that you have no control over?

I CAN TRANSFORM ANY TRAUMA THAT WAS PASSED DOWN TO ME.

I will treat myself with

____

How do you define
being "productive"?

Is your productivity linked to
your worth and/or value?

I DESERVE
PEOPLE
WHO
ADD TO
ME.

It's
normal to
experience
intense
emotion,
and I am
capable of

____

How do you define "balance"?

Is your definition of balance sustainable?
Is it realistic for this season of your life?

I DON'T
NEED
ANYONE'S
PERMISSION
TO HEAL.

I can thrive in the midst of

____

Describe your "ideal self."
Describe your "less-than-ideal self."

What makes you "ideal"?
What makes you "less than ideal"?

I DON'T HAVE TO DO IT ALL, ALL AT THE SAME TIME.

I survived

Do you have hobbies?
If so, what are they? If not, why?

What's your relationship with
trying new things?

THIS IS MY NARRATIVE AND I'M THE MAIN CHARACTER.

I am
confident
that

____

Sometimes we use untrue or limiting language to describe ourselves and/or our experiences. For example: "I'll never be good enough" or "I can't do this because I could fail." What are some of the false and/or limiting narratives you tell yourself?

What makes them seem real/true?

I DON'T
HAVE TO
PARTICIPATE
IN OTHER
PEOPLE'S
WARPED
VERSION
OF ME.

My love is

___

In what areas of your life could you show up for yourself more?

What would showing up more require?

I GIVE
MYSELF
PERMISSION
TO ACCEPT
WHO I AM
IN THIS
MOMENT.

The love
I have for
myself
can

____

Describe the activities you participate in that make you feel "good" (physically, emotionally, mentally, spiritually).

How often do you engage in those activities? What challenges/barriers get in the way if you don't get to engage as often as you'd like?

IT'S
OKAY TO
LET IT GO,
PUT IT
DOWN,
OR
PUT IT
BACK.

I can cultivate healthy

____

How do you feel when you ask for help/support and you don't get it, or it's not up to the standard that you'd give it, or it's just simply not what you asked for?

Do you specify the support/help you need?
Do you consider your audience
(that is, who you're asking)?
Explain.

I CAN
ACKNOWLEDGE
WHAT'S NOT
IN MY CONTROL
AND FOCUS
ON WHAT IS
IN MY CONTROL
AND RELISH
IN THAT.

I can count on myself to

____

Does something you do or try have to be perfect in your mind before you execute it? Explain.

If it didn't go exactly as planned, is it a complete failure? Are you a failure? Explain.

I CAN
USE THIS
MOMENT
TO GIVE
MYSELF
SOME
GRACE.

I am
allowed
to

____

Do you find it difficult to consider your strengths during adversity and challenges? Explain.

Are your strengths often overshadowed by your mistakes/limitations? Explain.

I DON'T HAVE TO USE THIS MOMENT TO WORRY ABOUT THE FUTURE.

Are you often in environments or spaces that lead you to feel drained? Describe the environment. Are there elements that could be removed? Are there elements that could be added?

Are these environments or spaces that you must be in? If so, do you replenish that energy before going back in? If not, why do you keep going back?

MY NEEDS ARE JUST AS IMPORTANT AS ANYONE ELSE'S.

Do you make space for the things/people that nourish you?

If so, how? If not, why?

I HAVE
EVERYTHING
I NEED TO
NAVIGATE
THIS... AND
IF I DON'T,
I'M CAPABLE
OF FIGURING
IT OUT.

How often do you say,
"I'll just do it my damn self"
or a version of that?

Do you think, "Well, when I do it, it's just better"?
But what gets sacrificed in the process?
Maybe you're okay with a little sacrifice, but what happens when those little sacrifices add up?

MY HAPPINESS, PEACE, AND CONTENTMENT ARE NOT CONDITIONAL. I HAVE THE POWER TO ACCESS IT ANYTIME.

How do you connect with yourself?

Is the connection often lost?
If so, how do you restore it?
How do you want to sustain it?

I CAME
INTO THIS
SPACE AND
I'M CAPABLE
OF REMOVING
MYSELF FROM
THIS SPACE
IF NEED BE.

Describe your relationship with perfection.

Describe your relationship with imperfection.

IT'S
OKAY
IF I'M
NOT
OKAY.

What's your relationship with fear?

What could happen if you did things *while* you are feeling fear?

I'M
COMPETENT
ENOUGH TO
NAVIGATE
THROUGH
THIS.

Do you often apologize for how you feel?

If so, why?

I'M HUMAN
AND I'M
ALLOWED
TO HAVE
HUMAN
EXPERIENCES.

Describe your day-to-day stressors.

How do they impact you?

I CAN GIVE
OTHERS
ACCESS
TO ME AND
I CAN ALSO
REMOVE
ACCESS.

Describe your more extreme stressors.
(You may not experience these daily or even often, but when you do... what are they?)

What's the impact? Do you recover?
Is recovery necessary for you?
Is recovery intentional? How do you recover?

I DON'T HAVE TO REMAIN IN SITUATIONS WHERE I DON'T FEEL SAFE.

Fill in the blank for the following statements:

When I'm in survival mode, it feels like...

When I'm in survival mode, it seems like...

When I'm thriving, it feels like...

When I'm thriving, it seems like...

Have you adjusted a little too well to being in survival mode, so much so that it's the only place you operate from? What would it take for you to thrive a little? A lot?

MY TIME IS
IMPORTANT.

Do you consider the validation of others more important than your own?

What would happen if you listened to your validation first and more often?

MY SPACE
IS SACRED.

What's your relationship with patience?

Do you practice patience with yourself?
If so, how? If not, what gets in the way?

I AM THE
PROTECTOR
OF MY
ENERGY.

Recall a time when you noticed that you were overextending yourself. What was that like for you? Did you stop as soon as you noticed? If so, what did it take for you to stop? If not, what would it have taken for you to stop?

How do you recover emotionally, mentally, physically, spiritually after you stop overextending yourself?

I WILL MAKE
TIME AND SPACE
TO ACKNOWLEDGE
AND CELEBRATE
MYSELF AND MY
ACCOMPLISHMENTS.

What are the signs that indicate you're about to overextend yourself?

If you are someone who automatically says "Yes" when asked to help someone else, what would it be like to use phrases such as... "Let me check my calendar," "Let me make sure I have the space for that," and/or "I'm not sure, but I'll get back with you" instead? What could your go-to phrase sound like?

THIS MOMENT
IS BRAND NEW,
AND I CAN
CHOOSE WHAT
I BRING INTO IT
AND TAKE
OUT OF IT.

Do you think you deserve to be celebrated? Why? Why not?

How do you celebrate yourself?

I AM
CONSTANTLY
EVOLVING.

Do you reach milestones and move on?
Do you achieve your goals and move on?

What would happen if you paused, relished, took stock, rested, and celebrated before proceeding?

I CAN
LOVE
MYSELF
WITHOUT
CONDITIONS.

What brings you peace?

What can you remove from your environment/space right now that's obstructing your peace? What can you add to your environment right now that gives you peace (it doesn't have to be anything big)?

MY
WELL-BEING
IS
IMPORTANT.

Do you often expect others to anticipate your needs/wants...to read your mind? Explain.

What is your self-talk if those needs go unmet?

I HAVE THE OPTION OF CHOOSING MYSELF.

What are some things that you can say and do to restore yourself emotionally, mentally, physically, and spiritually?

What are some things that you can say and do to encourage yourself emotionally, mentally, physically, and spiritually during challenging moments?

I AM
CAPABLE
OF
HEALTHY
COPING.

In what relationships or spaces do you feel comfortable advocating for yourself? In what relationships or spaces do you feel less comfortable advocating for yourself? Describe.

What could be added to those relationships or spaces that could help you feel more comfortable in advocating for yourself?

I AM
CAPABLE OF
COMMUNICATING
MY NEEDS.

I CAN
TAKE CARE
OF MY
EMOTIONAL,
PHYSICAL,
MENTAL,
AND SPIRITUAL
NEEDS.

I WILL
LISTEN
TO MY
BODY
MORE.

I AM
CAPABLE
OF
CHANGE.

I DON'T HAVE
TO MINIMIZE
MYSELF IN THE
PRESENCE OF
SOMEONE
WHO I BELIEVE
IS ON A
DIFFERENT
LEVEL FROM ME.

I DON'T
HAVE TO
RUSH...
THIS
MOMENT IS
SUFFICIENT.

EVERYTHING DOESN'T HAVE TO BE HARD.

EVERYTHING
DOESN'T
HAVE TO
BE A
STRUGGLE.

Journal Prompts

We often get so caught up in our day that we either forget or don't realize when we've done something to take care of ourselves. It's important for you to know how you're navigating your days, especially if you're trying to design the best way to take care of you. You'll notice that each journal prompt begins with "Today."

Use these journal prompts to help you stay present and acknowledge the many ways you take care of yourself.

Today,
I felt proud when I...

Today,
I made a decision based
on what I needed,
and I feel...

Today,
I trusted myself and I...

Today,
I __________ and I didn't feel guilty about it...

Today,
I took a moment for
myself and I...

Today,
I used my voice and I...

Today,
I had an opportunity
to __________ and I...

Today, I set a boundary and I...

Today,
I needed support, I asked for it, and it allowed me to...

Today,
I made a decision and
I didn't like the outcome,
so I can/will...

Today, I chose to...

Today,
I felt motivated when I...

Today,
I acknowledged...

Today,
I felt empowered when...

Today, I felt calm when...

Today,
I felt in control when...

Today,
I felt out of control when...

Today,
I tried something new
and I feel...

Today,
I was able to shift my
perspective and I feel...

Today,
I didn't allow false narratives
to run me and I feel...

Today,
I didn't fall into the trap of
how others perceive me
and I feel...

Today,
I leaned into my authenticity,
and it allowed me to...

Today,
I considered myself more,
and I...

Today,
I didn't consider myself
as much and I...

www.ingramcontent.com/pod-product-compliance
Ingram Content Group UK Ltd.
Pitfield, Milton Keynes, MK11 3LW, UK
UKHW061952290726
14090UKWH00021B/1183

9 798218 187248